PRESENTED TO

_____

FROM

_____

DATE

_____

THE
BIGGEST
STORY

THE BIGGEST STORY

HOW THE SNAKE CRUSHER
BRINGS US BACK TO THE GARDEN

KEVIN DEYOUNG

ILLUSTRATED BY
DON CLARK

CROSSWAY · WHEATON, ILLINOIS

The Biggest Story

Text copyright © 2015 by Kevin DeYoung

Illustration copyright © 2015 by Don Clark

Published by Crossway

   1300 Crescent Street

   Wheaton, Illinois 60187

Published in association with the literary agency of Wolgemuth & Associates, Inc.

Cover design & illustration: Don Clark for Invisible Creature, Inc.

First printing 2015

Printed in China

Hardcover ISBN: 978-1-4335-4244-2

ePub ISBN: 978-1-4335-4247-3

PDF ISBN: 978-1-4335-4245-9

Mobipocket ISBN: 978-1-4335-4246-6

Library of Congress Cataloging-in-Publication Data

DeYoung, Kevin.

The biggest story / Kevin DeYoung.

pages cm

ISBN 978-1-4335-4244-2 (hc)

1. Bible Stories, English. I. Title.

BS551.3.D49 2015

220.95'05—dc23
                    2014007720

Crossway is a publishing ministry of Good News Publishers.

RRDS   27   26   25   24   23

16   15   14   13   12   11   10   9

Kevin DeYoung:
For Ian, Jacob, Elizabeth, Paul, Mary, and Benjamin,
with more love than you know.

Don Clark:
For Ella, Cash, and Flora,
my three greatest sources of inspiration.

TABLE OF

CONTENTS

NCE UPON A TIME there lived a man and a woman. They were the happiest people on the planet. True, they were the *only* people on the planet, but they were still terrifically happy.

Their names were Adam and Eve, and God made them. He made them in his image, little mirrors to reflect God's glory. And like everything else God made, he made them good.

It was a wonderful time to be God's children in God's wonderful world.

Unfortunately, things didn't stay happy and wonderful for long.

On one very bad day, Adam ate from the only tree God had declared off-limits. Adam failed. It was a terrible day, the second-worst day in the history of the world.

A snake had tricked Adam and Eve and told them a lie about the fruit. He said they would be like God if they ate it. But actually, the opposite was true. When they ate the fruit, they found themselves far away from God.

They had disobeyed God's word and believed the lie of that devilish Snake instead of the truth. Being near to God—and having him draw near to us—would not be easy any longer.

God was not happy with Adam and Eve. He wasn't happy with the Snake either. God put a curse on the man and the woman and the Snake and everything else.

He kicked Adam and Eve out of the garden Paradise he had made for them. It wasn't possible for a people who were so bad to live with a God who is so good.

They had to go.

But before they left, God made a promise. He promised that the evil Serpent, the Devil, would always be at war with Eve and her children.

Now that doesn't sound like a very nice promise—that bad guys and good guys would fight all the time. Who wants to be in a war that never ends?

But here's where the good part of the promise comes in: God promised that one of Eve's children would, someday, eventually, sooner or later, crush the head of that nasty Snake.

Nobody knew when or how, but she would have a child to put things right.

SADLY, THINGS GOT A LOT WORSE before they got any better.

Adam and Eve had several kids, including two brothers named Cain and Abel. Abel trusted God, but Cain did not. And when God accepted Abel's gift and not Cain's, Cain got very angry— so angry, so hurt, and so jealous that he killed his brother.

It was the first murder in history, but it wouldn't be the last.

Things were not the way they were supposed to be. Everything fell apart after sin entered the world.

Things got so bad so fast that God decided to start over. The people on the earth were terribly wicked in their hearts, all the time, every day, nonstop.

They didn't deserve to enjoy God's world anymore.

So God took it from them.

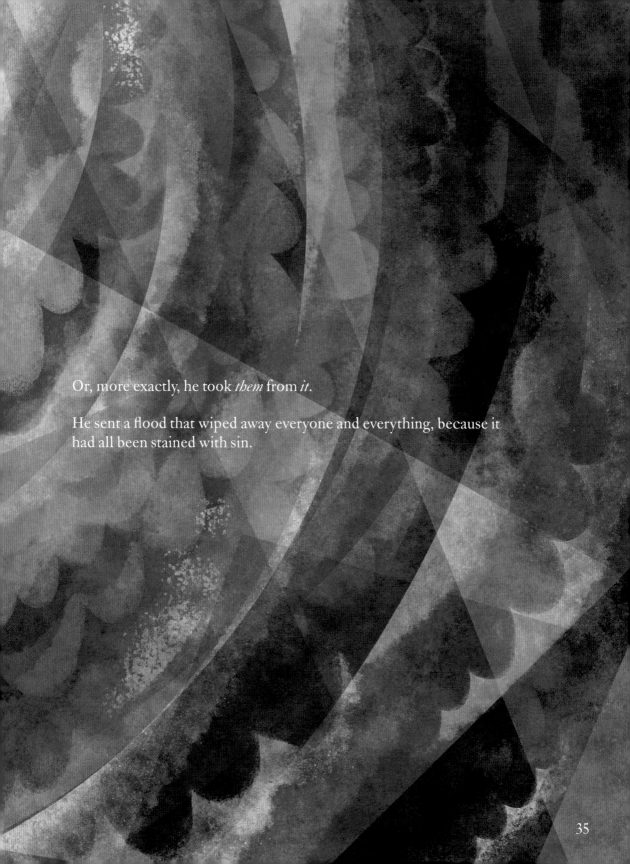

Or, more exactly, he took *them* from *it*.

He sent a flood that wiped away everyone and everything, because it had all been stained with sin.

Well, almost everything. God saved one family on the earth—one family that trusted him and believed what he said.

Noah and his wife, and their sons and their wives, were spared. They lived for a lot of days with a lot of animals in a big boat called an ark. It rained and rained.

God was going to start over with his creation. He was angry with the world that hated him, but he was still at work to save the world that he loved. That's why he rescued Noah and his family.

God wanted to give his people another shot. God was going to start over with a new world, and Noah was going to be a new kind of Adam.

The problem was that Noah was *too much* like the first Adam. It didn't take long after they got out of the boat for Noah to do some pretty bad stuff himself.

He trusted God enough to build an ark when everyone laughed at him, but it turns out he could be just as foul as everybody else. Even one of Noah's sons got cursed, just like everything got cursed back in the garden.

History was repeating itself. Whether it was Adam or Noah, the first world in the beginning or the second world after the flood, people just couldn't get things right.

One time, a whole bunch of people got together to build a giant tower. They thought they could build all the way up to heaven. But it must not have been all that big because God had to come down just to see it.

And when God saw it, he was not pleased. Everyone was working together, which was okay, but they weren't working for God, and that was not okay. They were trying to show how smart and impressive they could be all on their own. They thought they didn't need God. So God mixed up all their languages and scattered the people all over the place.

Things were still not going well in the world God had made. Thankfully, God was still not done saving his people.

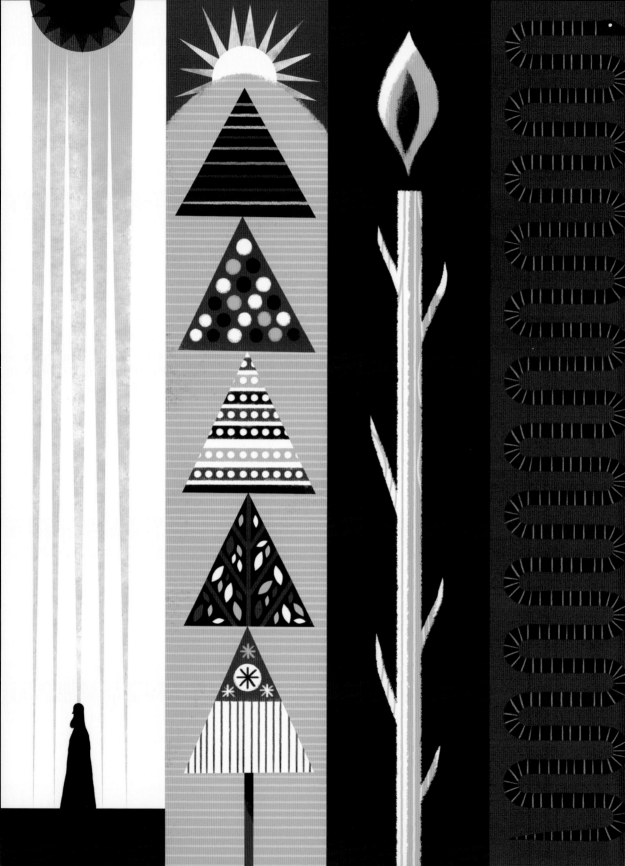

 OT TOO LONG AFTER the whole tower business, God called a man named Abraham to leave his home and go to a new country. (Actually his name was Abram at this point, but everyone remembers him as Abraham.)

When God called Abraham, he made a lot of big promises.

He promised to bless Abraham and to bless everyone who blessed Abraham.

He promised to curse everyone who cursed Abraham. He promised Abraham a land and a child.

God promised that Abraham would be the father of a great nation and that all nations would be blessed through him.

Pretty much, all the blessing that God wanted to give Adam and Eve, he promised to Abraham. And the best part? This time God was going to do everything himself to make sure Abraham got his blessing.

You might think that God wanted to bless Abraham because he was such a swell guy. But Abraham didn't know God at all when God called him. And even after he got the call and all these promises, Abraham could still be a liar and a bit of a scaredy-cat.

Abraham's life had a lot of ups and downs. But he had two things going for him—the only two things, it turns out, that really matter: God's promise to bless him and Abraham's belief in God's promise.

That's all Abraham had. Which was a good deal, because it was all he needed.

At times, it looked as if God wasn't going to keep his promises to Abraham. For one thing, it was about a hundred years before Abraham and his wife Sarah (who used to be called Sarai) had a baby named Isaac (who, thankfully, was always called Isaac).

And then when the baby grew into a boy, God told Abraham to kill him. That must have seemed like a not-so-funny way to make a great nation out of Abraham, but Abraham listened to God anyway. And at the last second, God gave Abraham a ram to sacrifice instead of his beloved son.

It was God's way of saying, "I'll take care of the rescuing. Just trust me."

Eventually Isaac grew up, got married, and had some kids of his own. Twins to be exact—Esau and Jacob.

God picked Jacob to get the blessing even though he was the younger brother and wasn't supposed to get the blessing. But God is God, so he gets to pick.

Jacob had twelve sons, and this time it was the fourth son, Judah, who wound up with the best blessing. Jacob told Judah that a lion of a leader would come from his family.

Great blessings. But not-so-great people.

Isaac was sort of a weakling.

Jacob was a selfish trickster.

And Judah did such dumb stuff, we don't even want to talk about it.

And yet, again and again, God kept his promises all the same. He blessed the whole lot of them despite themselves.

Maybe the Snake Crusher would still come from the gnarled branches of the Abraham-Isaac-Jacob family tree.

SEVERAL HUNDRED YEARS after God's promise to Abraham, it looked like things had gotten way off track.

When God told Abraham to leave his home, he promised to give him a new land in Canaan. It was going to be a great land. It was supposed to remind God's people of the garden they once had. It would be sweet and refreshing with plenty of milk and honey.

But Abraham and his sons never really possessed the land they were promised. And now it was four hundred years later, and they were slaves in Egypt.

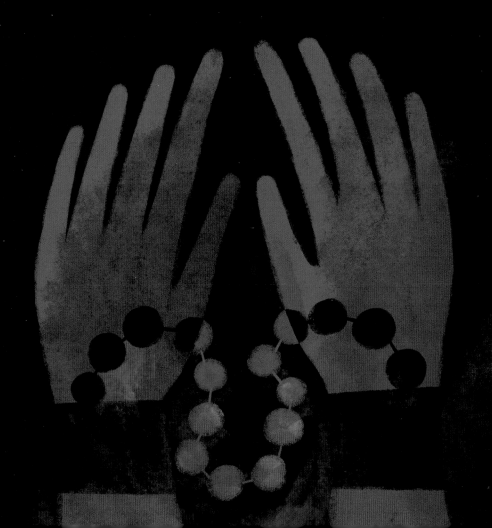

How Abraham's family got to Egypt is a long story, but here's the short version:

They went to Egypt because there was a famine in Canaan, and when they got to Egypt, Jacob's sons found their long-lost brother Joseph, who helped get them food and a place to live even though he was there because his ten older brothers had been jealous and sold him into slavery after they almost killed him because of his fancy coat.

(I told you it was a long story.)

Well, delivering them from famine was one thing. That's when Israel's family was still pretty small. (Israel, by the way, was Jacob's new name. I guess everyone needed two names back then.) But hundreds of years later the family was *huge*.

How would God save a couple million people from slavery?

It's not like he could just turn the Nile River into blood and send frogs and gnats and flies and disease and boils and hail and locusts and darkness and death until the king of Egypt let them go!

Actually, that's exactly what God did.

God raised up Moses to deliver his people—but in reality God did all the work.

He sent the plagues.

He led the people with fire and cloud.

He made the sea turn to dry land so the Israelites could walk through, and he turned the dry land back to sea when the Egyptians tried to cross over.

It seemed that no matter what the Israelites did or what everyone else did to them, God always found a way to save his people.

T WAS A VERY GOOD THING God was always rescuing his people. Because it seemed that no matter how many times God saved his people, the Israelites were never quite safe from themselves.

See, after God delivered his people from Egypt, he gave them a lot of commandments. This wasn't to punish them but to help and protect them.

They were good commandments. And if they obeyed the commandments, God's people would be blessed. There would be food and children and long life and protection and a new home.

It would be just like they were in Paradise again. That's where God wanted to lead them all along, back to the garden.

But if they didn't obey, there would be curses, just like the ones that fell on Adam and Eve and the Serpent.

As you might have guessed, the people didn't do so well obeying God's commands. And after Moses and his helper Joshua died, they disobeyed even more.

They ignored the most important commands, and when they did work hard at some rules—like getting their sacrifices right—they didn't really obey those rules from the heart. They just checked them off their list and forgot about the more important commands.

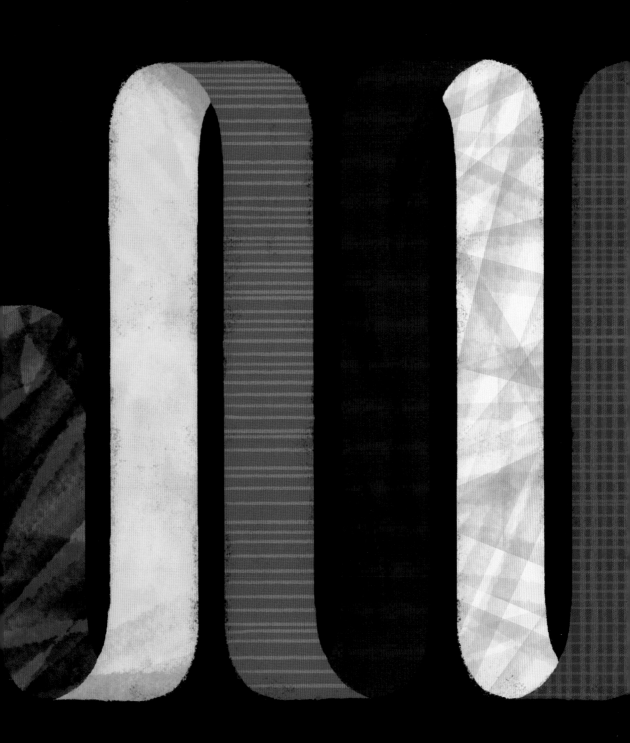

Not that God's people deserved it, but God finally gave them their Promised Land.

God did the work to get them in, but God's people didn't do the work to drive everyone else out.

This caused a lot of trouble for the Israelites . . .

They constantly had enemies to fight. And worse, they constantly had to fight the temptation to be just like their enemies.

Sometimes things would go well for Israel—when they had a good leader and when they obeyed—but most often things went poorly.

God gave the Israelites rules (but they didn't follow them).

God made his dwelling among them (but they didn't act like they wanted him to stick around).

God sent prophets (but Israel didn't listen).

God provided priests (but the priests didn't know how to be holy).

Later, God gave them kings (but the kings were a royal pain).

Israel was a mess.

Of course, God still had his promises to keep. But most days it was hard to imagine how anyone could save this stubborn people.

It would have been even harder to imagine how the Promised Man could come from *among* this people.

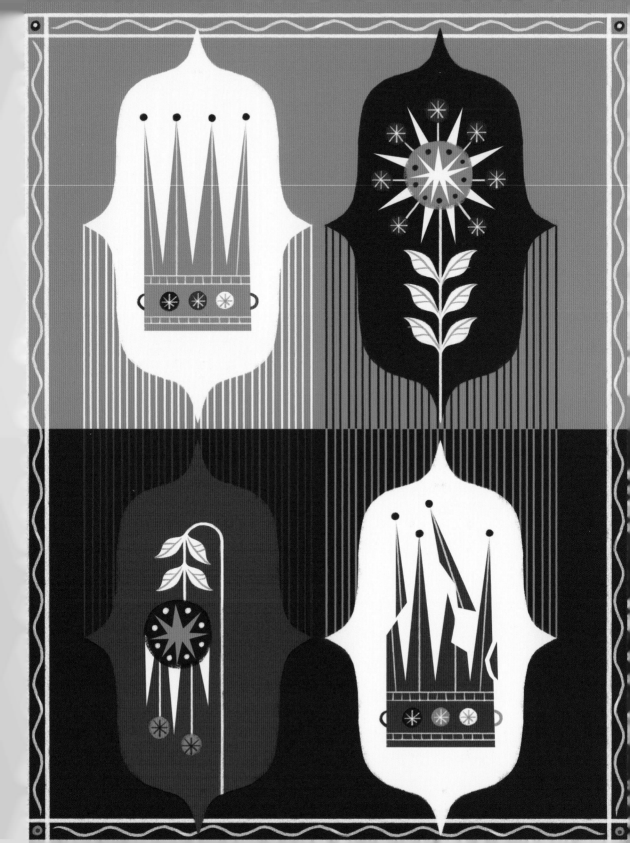

GOD'S PEOPLE HAD A HARD TIME not copying everyone else around them. This was especially true when it came to having a king.

Although God warned them how bad kings could be, they just had to have one. So, eventually, God gave them a king (be careful what you ask for—you just might get it).

The first king was Saul. He was very impressive height-wise, and pretty disappointing in every other way.

The second monarch, young David from Bethlehem, was definitely much better. In fact, before we get to *the* King, there's almost no one more important than King David.

When David wasn't busy sinning (which he did in some really big ways), he was a good, wise, merciful king. Many good things happened to God's people when David was in charge. They were victorious and prosperous and blessed.

But the best thing that happened was what God promised *would* happen. God told David that he would always have a son to sit on the throne. He promised David an everlasting kingdom.

This was good news for David, and even better news for God's people. It meant that God had not forgotten the guarantee he made in the garden. A deliverer was on his way. And now everyone who had ears to hear knew he would be a son of David.

But the next son of David was not the one they were looking for.
Solomon started off on the right foot, but he ended up tripping quite
spectacularly.

After Solomon, the kingdom split in two, with Israel in the North and
Judah in the South. Neither kingdom was very good.

God punished Israel first, then Judah.

In the course of four hundred years God's people would go from top dog to dog food. They had been kicked out of their Promised Land just like Adam and Eve had been kicked out of their Paradise. And worst of all, David's house and David's throne were no more.

The future looked bleak, especially for the promises of God.

BELIEVE IT OR NOT,
God's promises hadn't gone anywhere.

In fact, God kept on making more promises all the time.

God promised that the Snake Crusher—Abraham's child, Judah's lion, David's son—would come from Bethlehem.

God promised he would be born of a virgin.

God promised a messenger to prepare the way.

God promised that the Deliverer would die and live again and be a light to the nations.

God promised lots of amazing things.

But Israel was too busy disobeying God's commands and ignoring God's warnings to notice.

God sent miraculous prophets like Elijah and Elisha, and rebuking prophets like Amos and Malachi, and sad prophets like Jeremiah, and good news prophets like Isaiah.

It didn't matter which ones God sent or how many, the people never listened. Not for very long, anyway.

And so one day it happened: God stopped sending the prophets.

No more warnings. No more direction. No more word from the Lord. Only silence—for four hundred years.

God had sent prophets, priests, and kings. He started out with Adam and started over with Noah. He chose Abraham, Isaac, and Jacob. He gave Moses the Law. He sent Israel judges. He raised up deliverers. He conquered enemies. He provided sacrifices. He lived among his people in a tent and in a temple.

God gave them every opportunity and ten thousand chances, but still sin and the Serpent seemed to be winning.

Until . . . all of a sudden, they lost.

AFTER ALL THESE DOWNS—and not too many ups—we come to a manger in the little town of Bethlehem.

This is where we meet the new Adam, the child of Abraham, the Son of David. It's with the stinky shepherds and the singing angels where we see the real Deliverer, the real Judge, the real Conqueror.

No one understood it completely at the time, but when Mary pushed out that baby, God pushed into the world the long-expected Prophet, Priest, and King.

God gave his people a new law, a new temple, and a new sacrifice. Best of all, he gave his people a new beginning. Just as he promised.

Of course, some things were different than people had expected. The stable with the animals and the scandal with unmarried Mary were surprises to most folks.

The miracles were remarkable.

The teaching was unlike anything anyone had ever heard.

The bumbling band of hand-picked disciples—that was curious.

But the biggest surprise to everyone was that the Chosen One of God was chosen by God to die.

It just didn't seem right that the One destined to crush the Serpent would be crushed himself. So when Jesus, the Christ, the Son of the living God, died on the cross that Friday afternoon, it seemed a shocking evil beyond belief.

And it was. The worst thing that's ever happened in the world.

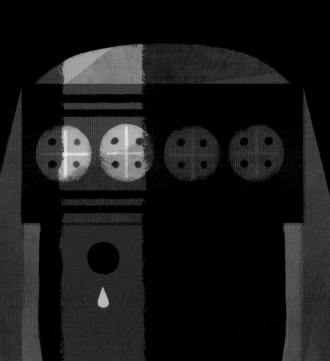

But it was also the best thing that's ever happened in the world. Just as we would expect from God. And just as God planned it.

We break promises, so God keeps his.

We run from God, so he comes to us.

We suffer for sin, so the Savior suffers for us.

Our story is the story of God doing what we can't, in order to make up for us doing what we shouldn't. The Christ suffers for our sin, that we might share in his sinlessness.

And so deliverers are born to die. Things fall apart so they can come together. God kicks his own people out of Paradise and then does whatever it takes to bring them back again.

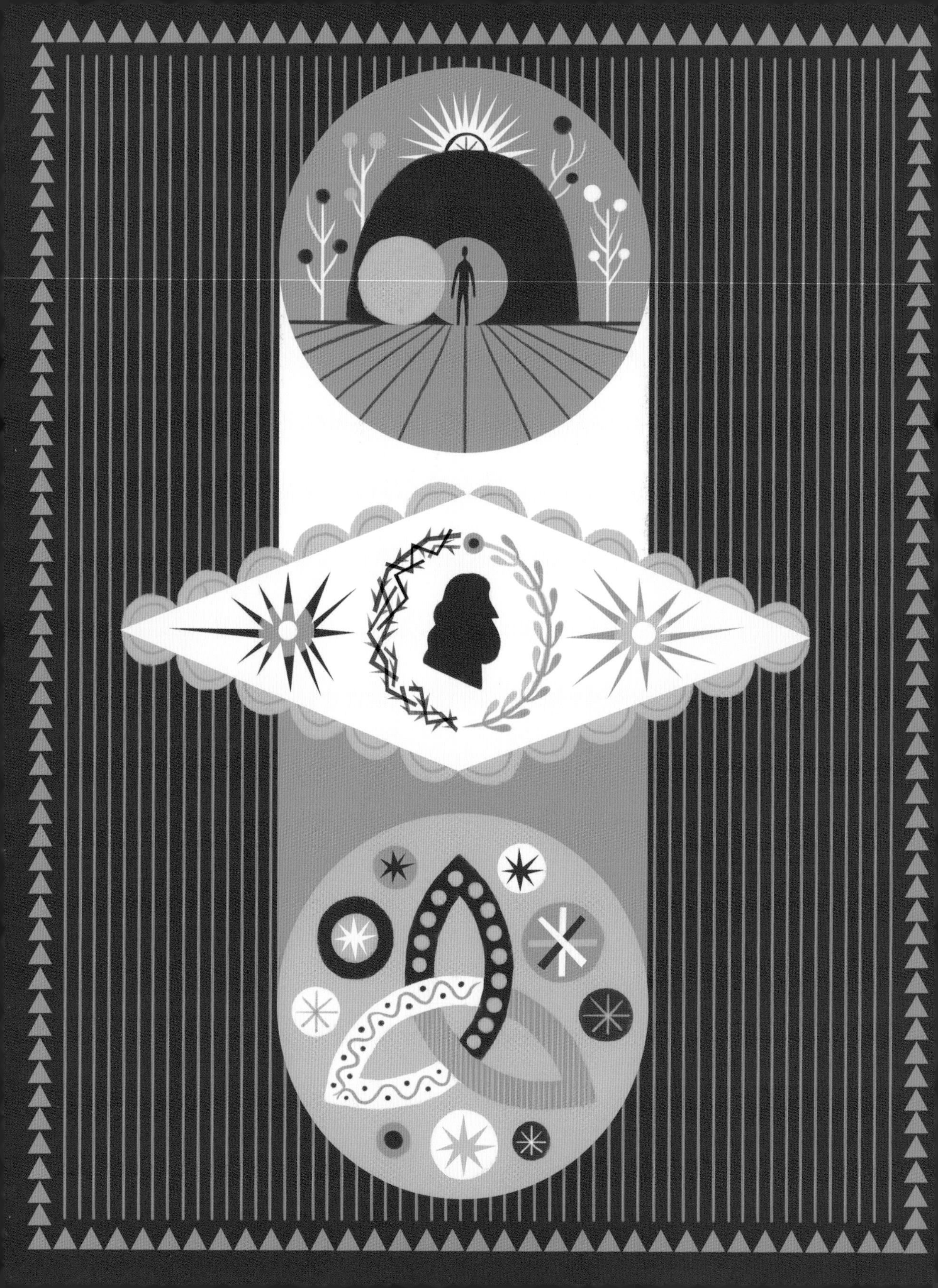

AS YOU MAY HAVE HEARD, and should definitely tell someone else, the Snake Crusher who died on the cross didn't stay dead.

He couldn't.

Death had no claim on him.

The Devil had no case against him.

And sin had no wages for him that he couldn't pay.

Jesus just couldn't stay dead, and God just wouldn't let him rot in the tomb. So on the third day, God raised him from the dead.

HE IS

RISEN

A whole bunch of people saw him and ate with him and told their friends that he was really alive.

Forty days later God lifted him into the sky and gave him the seat of honor at his right hand.

And you know what the Snake Crusher did next?

Because his work was done, he sat down. And God gave him the name above all names, so that at the name of Jesus everybody and everything would start to sing and shout and worship.

Then, just to make things even better and to make good on even more promises, God the Father and God the Son sent the best present of all time down to earth.

They gave the gift of the Holy Spirit. And because of the Spirit, we can have power and peace and the presence of Christ with us all the time.

AS YOU CAN TELL, this story is a big story. In fact, it's the Biggest Story.

It's a familiar story to some of us. It's a true story for all of us. But we haven't seen the end of the story—not yet.

We live in the beginning of the end of the story that we are still in the middle of. We know it's not the end because we haven't made it back to the garden.

We get glimpses of the garden here and there—in our hearts, in our families, in the church. But anyone who loves this story longs to see the One who is the center of the story.

The Snake Crusher is coming back again to wipe away all the bad guys and wipe away every tear. He's coming to make a new beginning and to finish what he started. He's coming to give us the home we once had and might have forgotten that we lost.

So keep waiting for him. Keep believing in him. Keep trusting that the story isn't over yet. God's promises never fail and the Promised One never disappoints.

One day we will see him. One day we will be with him. One day there will be nothing but the best days, day after day after day after day.

And forever and ever it will be a wonderful time to be God's children in God's wonderful world.

A NOTE TO PARENTS

The Bible is a big story made up of lots of smaller stories. Many children (and not a few adults) learn to see the Bible as nothing but a nice collection of all these smaller stories. Here a story about Abraham. There a story about Daniel. And in there somewhere are familiar stories about Christmas and Easter. Our kids can become acquainted with many Bible stories without ever grasping the Biggest Story that makes sense of all the others.

This book began as a Christmas sermon for my church. I wanted to tell the familiar advent story in a way that was fresh and faithful to the biblical text. I tried to deliver the message like I was reading a book—a book for children sitting by the fire on Christmas morning. Alas, I had no fireplace in the pulpit that Sunday and no children gathered at my feet! But I hoped someday to carry the story past the Christmas narrative and find a gifted illustrator who could make the sweet gospel story sparkle as it should.

Some of the imagery in *The Biggest Story* may be unfamiliar to children. Even parents and teachers may have to strain a bit to understand the allusions. Most of the book is a straightforward—and hopefully a playful and elegant—retelling of the biblical plotline with a good dose of the usual stories about Adam and Eve, Abraham, Moses, David, and of course, Jesus. But lurking in the background are a couple of big themes you don't want to overlook.

First, I've tried to emphasize how Jesus is not only the Savior for our sins, but also the fulfillment of a long line of prophecies, patterns, and predictions. For example, in chapter 8, I note that Jesus embodies the three offices in ancient Israel: prophet, priest, and king. I also reference Jesus as the fulfillment of Israel's worship. He is a new law, a new temple, and a new and final sacrifice for his people. Most significantly, I speak of Jesus throughout the book as a new Adam. This is important New Testament imagery (Rom. 5:12-21; 1 Cor. 15:45). Every human being belongs to either the first Adam or the second Adam. What Adam failed to do in sinning in Eden, Jesus Christ accomplished by his perfect life and sacrificial death.

Second, you'll notice the theme of "garden" looms large. It's not a coincidence that the biblical story starts in a garden (Genesis 1) and ends in a garden (Revelation 22). The Biggest Story is the story of rebels kicked out of their home and longing to return. The fundamental problem that the Bible answers is how a holy God can dwell in the midst of a sinful people. God kicked Adam and Eve out of the garden of Eden because his eyes were too pure to look upon human sin and corruption. It was for the same reason he sent the flood in Noah's day and exiled Israel from the land of Canaan. And it's for this reason God sent his Son to die on a cross. We need redemption. We need forgiveness. We need the Promised One to lead us to our promised home.

I pray that for some this book may become a treasured "member" of the family, a book that you and your children, or you and your students, keep coming back to time and time again. Not because the pictures on these pages are so striking (though they are), or because the story I've written is so special, but because the Bible's biggest story—the story of our snake-crushing King and our destined-to-die Deliverer—is the best story that's ever been told.